MW01228567

SPREAD YOUR WINGS

A Collection of Soulful Poems

Let's get ready to flow into some reading like a water faucet drip….

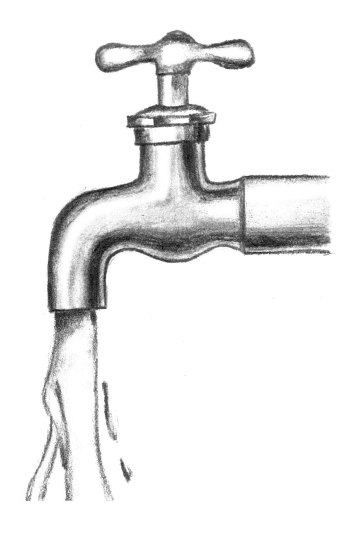

SPREAD YOUR WINGS

A Collection of Soulful Poems

by
Dr. Melissa M. Gillespie
Stylysa

ISBN: 9798874439798

The poems *Friends, they come and they go - Parts 1* and *2*, *Martin Luther King, Jr.*, and *Life* were written by Stephen C. Telford and are used by permission.

For information on this book, please contact:
Dr. Melissa M. Gillespie at stylysa@icloud.com or stylysa@ymail.com.

WrightStuf Consulting

Printed in the United States of America

Words of encouragement

_____

_____

Autographed by

Dr. Melissa M. Gillespie

Stylysa the Poet

Dedication

To my first-born son, Stephen and my daughter, Miracle, always remember these words from your momma. (Alpha and Omega kids)

Always put the Lord first in everything you do in life, watch doors open for you in your season, and thank God for the ones he closed that weren't meant for you to go through.

Never stop dreaming for the best in your life, think out of the box, reinvent yourself as needed, and make your dreams come true. Never allow anyone to put limitations on you because what God has for you is for you.

"A mother's heart beats are her children."

Three of my favorite scriptures for 2 of my favorite children!

Mark 11:24

Proverbs 18:16

Jeremiah 29:11

Stephen

Miracle

Table of Contents

Dedication

Acknowledgements

Opening Prayer

Acknowledgements

I first would like to thank my Lord, for EVERYTHING!

My mom, Eleanor Crews, you did a marvelous job raising 3 beautiful women, my sisters Janet & Angela.

My Alpha and Omega children, Stephen and Miracle, Momma loves you both always and forever.

To all my family and friends along my pathway in this journey called life, Yvette, friends since elementary school, and Vanessa Miracle's godmother.

Special thanks to Shia Millen for all the beautiful pictures in my book.

"DMV, Chocolate City baby, with Go-Go music and mumbo sauce."

A special thanks to the Ministers who spoke over my life that I would produce books from pen to paper; here it is!

LAST BUT NOT LEAST, I LIKE TO THANK ALL MY ENEMIES.COM

To God be all the Glory!

Opening Prayer

That all the readers would be Blessed

Spiritually

Practically

Humorously

In a soulful kind of way

For the soul

From a Soul Sista

"Stylysa"

Part I

Situationships

A Love Poem

He told me he loved me. He showed me he loved me.

This is a love poem of someone who told me that they would never leave me or forsake me Deuteronomy 31:6

I walked away from Him and tried others, but when I came back to my first love, H was still there with some of my gifts, waiting for me to receive them, you know them, love, peace, and joy, and yes indeed, I was in need.

I thank you, Lord. You see, it was me who left you, but baby, I'm back with a strong attack to get what's mine from the Lord.

You see, the gifts from the others don't dare to compare the perfume in the bottle was a different smell for the sweet, sweet smell with Him without no bottle, and His food that He gave me to taste and see was like a buffet for me wanting more.

You see it took a lot to calm me down, but with the right one in my life, who is Jesus Christ, I don't mind, but I heard some of you called on Him because I know I still do because I know He'll be a friend until the end.

I'm all up in His face because it's a beautiful thing to know the eyes of the Lord are on the righteous, and His ears hear the cry of his people, and to know His voice, oh His voice strikes with flashes of lightning.

If any of you talk to my friend, tell Him, I'm still seeking His face, and His gifts are far better than the others, and that's just some of His gifts, and it's not even my birthday.

A Wedding Day

There goes the bride, all dressed in white to meet her groom, who will groom her with his love, the love of Christ, and we all know that will be alright.

To be in love is a beautiful way to express yourself to your groom when you said those I do's.

To be in love is like a walk in the park, and how free it feels when it's just you two when you go down the aisle to say your do's.

To meet your Bride was a surprise, because the walk to your will only be for you to take her hand, her heart and that's just a start of what God has in store when she walked thru those doors.

Remember the rules before you said those I do's that today is your day to express your love and the love of Christ to one another, so when you both tell your story on your special day, don't forget to give God the Glory His way!

Universal Love

Love is a universal story, and I'm the sista that's going to tell it to you while I am still in my??

You C, your game is not up to par, just like Shaq shooting at the foul line for the hoop. The only difference is you don't have no loot.

You C, I can be the sista that runs your water in that jacuzzi tub and gives you that nice body rub and, after that, a nice hot meal, but right now, you're not ready for a sista like me that keeps it real.

I tell you what I need, you tell me what you want, but wait a minute, I forgot you don't have no means, greens, mola, basically you're broke, so tell it to some other female folk.

There was a time I used to cry, but I took on that Johnson and Johnson attitude and have no more tears here because it's only the Lord who I fear. I need a man that can say yes, we can, and not thinking life's a joke.
Sometimes I wonder will I fall in love again, then I take on that Jessie attitude and keep hope alive, because my Boaz could be right around the corner telling all truths, and no lies, and that will be a nice surprise for a sista that likes to keep it real.

Relationships

The saying goes like this: everybody wants to be like Mike. Forget Mike; I want to be like Christ.

Who wants to be like Mike when Mike don't even have it right unless he has a basketball in his hand now he says he's retired. I hope he get inspired to have a relationship with God with some of the free time on his mind.

Now, who do you want to be like?

Church folks come to Church all dressed up, but are they clothed in their right mind to praise the Divine.

A relationship with God will make you do some things and change your ways.

A relationship with God will make you sit thru 3 services and not think about Sunday dinner.

A relationship with God will have your face on the floor praising the Lord.

A relationship with God will let you know he don't bless no mess when your striving for his best.

A relationship with God will make you be at the Church door wanted more.

A relationship with God will keep your house tight, and make you love your mate right.

A relationship with God will make your kids act right and not be so uptight.

A relationship with God will make you wake up 3 and 5 in the morning seeking His Glory.

Where is your relationship with God?

I come with instructions

I'm not the season woman for some men because they refuse to see the real in me, so they just have to hear from me.
I think I'm a ray of sunshine, and if you can't get with that, hummm! You'll be left behind.

Trust is a must that has to be rooted in planted for me to see in you, just like a butterfly in transition of flying high, so, am I in the word of God.

You see, I put those players days behind me, so let me re-introduce you to the new coach, that don't have time for overtime, or foolish time, lying time, somebody else man time, broke no money time, live with your momma time, I just don't got time! But for a God-fearing man time, hmmm! I 'll make time!

I'm blowing the whistle on your game, because you have to be on the same frequency to be with me. Please don't play with this season woman, that carries a lot of ingredients inside of me, this red bone is like red pepper, a little spicy and bad to the bone, and just like salt that can raise your pressure, so can I without all that mouth and a bunch of lectures.
So, before you step to me, bring the right soldier man in front of me, and not a representative, not a counterfeit, because this redbone will shut it down and call it quits.

Part II

Stephen, Age 11

Friends, they come and they go - Part 1

Friends, they come and they go, but wait, didn't you know you may play at the beach or may play in the snow? You may have a little or a lot of friends. If you have a lot do you know their names?

Are your friend or friends good or bad?

They may want you to take liquor or want you to steal a snicker. You stole the snicker you're in jail now you want your mom and dad to get bail they won't do it now you pay the price for the next couple of months you're going to have water & rice.

If you just had said no, you wouldn't be in this mess, but instead you could've been blessed.

Friends, they come and they go!

By Stephen C. Telford - age 11

Friends, they come and they go - Part 2

I wrote a poem on how friends, they come and they go. Here goes part two just for you.

Would you let a guy or girl come between your friends and you? That person may break your heart, but you know you have a friend that will always be here for you, maybe till the very end.

A friend could change your life, good or bad; they can make U happy or sad or mad or change that all around.

For you to have a friendship you have to have a solid base, because some friends may be for real or two-faced.

When you grow up and one's a star, will the other be drinking at the bar?

Would you go to church together and worship the Lord? Would you go and be bored or be wondering about the football score?

If you stay in Church and school, your dreams will come true because, like I said, "Friends, they come and they go."

Stephen C. Telford - age 11

Martin Luther King Jr.

Dr. Martin Luther King Jr. was a good man he was a black leader and had a very good plan. He wasn't about guns, violence, and segregation all he wanted was freedom for the black nation.

He's like Rosa Parks won't give up her seat, because he knew the white system could be beat, he was a great leader who paved the way, that's why us black people are here today.

White people treated him bad and cruel, kids also loved him, because they get out of school, he was as big as everyone seem, because like he said, "I have a dream."

So, do I!

Stephen C. Telford - age 11

Life

What's the point of life? Give you a chance to do things right, learn to forgive instead of always looking for a fight. I read well, so I can write well, so my poems can flow well. Always challenge yourself, so your limits you can excel 'cause hard work always pays off even though it's hard to tell young in the eyes of many, but my mind is full of wisdom gotta lot of knowledge too, so maybe you should take a listen.

Never been one to judge.

Never been one to hold a grudge.

The devil tries to push me; too bad I never budge

With God on my side there's nothing out of my reach love being at church and hearing, "Preach, Pastor preach!" Never listen to the people who have nothing positive to say. Look at 'em, smile & tell 'em, "Have a nice day."

I been around the block a few times at such a young age 20 years old but somehow wise like a sage, still have a lot of learning to do from life, so I keep my eyes open even during the hard times. I pray and just keep hoping for better things to come for me and those around just pass me a microphone, so I can kick a poetry sound as I start to break it down for the people in every town at the end of the day you'll have no choice but to give me the crown.

*For being the poet that wrote it, this was a competition, but
I just stole it.
It's the best way to live life I promise you now, so trust in
the Lord do the right thing and I'm sure you'll see a
turnaround.*

Stephen C. Telford

Part III

The Journey

A Certain Woman God's Woman

When you're being looked at far and long and across the room or even in a dim room, and they still can't figure out who that lady is, well baby, tell them you're a certain woman, God's woman.

The woman that the husband and children call blessed, that's worth far more than rubies. A certain woman, a woman God can use no matter of her past being misused or abused because she's God's woman.

There's no residue on her because she has already been thru it; she learned a new dance to shake the haters off and to put God on. Her hand dance, back in the day just turned into God's praise dance for today.

Now when you see her coming, just hold the door open for her to go thru, because she's God's woman, a certain woman.

She is certain of who she is and whose she is because she knows that God is her all and all.

Now if you so happen to see this;

Wife, Mother
Submissive
Bless, Minister
Strong, Peacemaker
Meek, Spiritual

Type of woman who is phenomenal in everything she touches turns into gold type of woman. She might be the one you're looking at in the mirror, and men, if you're looking for her, pray on it because she is God's woman, a certain woman.

A Fresh Start

Trust, Delight, commit to the Lord, and watch your enemies drop to the floor if you wonder why you are set apart from your friends and family because God needs to do a fresh start in your heart so he can get the Glory, it's about the goodness of the Lord who you should adore, and not close the door for a fresh start.

A fresh start will allow you to do Psalms 37: 3,4,5 to trust, delight, and commit unto the Lord.

Trust- that you will be fed and not misled.

Delight- he will give you the desires of your heart with a fresh start.

Commit - Jesus will make your righteousness shine like the dawn.

If you say I don't need a fresh start, but examine your heart, can you pray with your mate, or do you think it's too late? Then, a fresh start does apply because God's word doesn't lie, so trust, delight, commit.

I'm single, doing ok. I don't have anyone driving me crazy, then you should have more time with the Lord and not being bored, so trust, delight, commit.

Shoot, I'm a teenager. This doesn't apply to me, but the last time I checked in John 6:9, that lad had 5 barley loaves and 2 small fish that fed the multitude, so lose that teenager attitude because you, too, can be used, so trust, delight, commit.

If there is anybody I missed for this fresh start, get the word in your heart to trust, delight, commit.

A wing and a hip swing

*I see a black man standing on the sidewalk eating a chicken wing; oh!
What a black man would do when you sista's walk past and let them
hips swing.*

*Please, black man, don't choke on that chicken wing because here
comes another sista with that same hip swing.*

*That swing will pass you by without a blink in your direction, so calm
down, your little friend, before you have an erection.*

*Black man, wipe that drool from your lips because sista girl already
down the street with those wide old hips.*

*So, have a Coke and a smile to wash down those chicken wings.
Maybe it would have helped if you put down that chicken wing and
had on a little bling bling!*

Are you ready for the attacks??

My heart is steadfast, oh Lord, and because of that, those attacks didn't last.

Many will attack you in their pride, but I will stand on God's word and not cry! In God whose word I praise in God I will trust I will not be afraid, so take up your shield and buckler and rise and fight the good fight of faith that's waiting among you. If you need to take refuge, it's in the shadow of his wings.

You will have troubles, but know that troubles don't last always, so knowing this, are you ready for the attacks? Did you put down your bottle filled with milk and pick up your sword to fight, or are you using your sword to cut your meat?

Get ready. You see, some will attract attacks in their lives, but know it's a good thing that's coming your way to make you strong soldiers for the Lord that fighting on the battlefield.

Get ready and be ready to be a part of the soldiers of the army of the Lord, get ready and be ready to gear up for the Lord and for the attacks, and know that God has your back because He got it like that.

Now, are you going to go back to your milk bottle or to get your sword and stand up for the Lord?

Blessed people attract attacks, so get ready!

An Invite

I don't say much, but I speak to Him every day. He's always there to help me to find my way, I don't deny our close association because He helps me out of my situation. If you haven't read the book of Revelation, you'll find that He's your only salvation.

So, if you have any doubts, just trade it in for a good old church shout!

This is my invitation to invite you to get a self-evaluation and see if He will get U out of your situation. Facebook, Instagram, Twitter, God can show up any place network to get His work done because I almost let go, but for every mountain, God has kept me, so don't abort the mission God has given you, especially if you don't get his permission to end the mission, even if you have to wait 9 months to push out your next assignment of life in this journey called Life.

ASK ME HOW I KNOW???? MIRACLE!

Ask yourself???

Watch your surroundings, or are your surroundings watching you?

Are you a people pleaser, or are the people pleasing you?

Can you stir yourself up, or do you have to be stirred up?

Can you praise Him in the midnight hour to see His glory of His power, or is your attitude just that sour?

Are you living by the crisis in your life or by Jesus Christ in your life?

Are you minding your business or busy in somebody else, you see, because some things are just God's business?

Before it gets late in the mid-night hour, say enough is enough, get the victory put on your Nike, and go home.

Before you have to cry out before temptation comes and consider your ways and remind yourself I'm still alive and thank God for the dawning of a new day for his grace, gain, and glory.

U C, it's in the details of the Bible because God can! So know there's nobody like Jesus who can please us, so know faith works because it requires waiting and works.

Wake up to a new order and be like-minded and like Christ and look to the hills which our help cometh from. Even if you have to go to the dwelling place sometimes, just tell yourself I won't complain, and have the believers fight because it's time to trust the Lord.

Black Man Rise

Be careful when U tell a black man to rise, ladies, when he comes out that shower after a long day of work laying on the bed smelling nice and good after washing off that last minute of dirt.

Do you say black man rise while crawling on top of him? Will it be a disappointment or a surprise?

Be careful when U tell a black man to rise because here comes a disconnection notice with 2 days to pay. Do you say black man rise, or do you get disconnected in the cable because he wasn't able?

Be careful when U tell a black man to rise when you laying out his suit to wear for the last time, saying to yourself I could have made him an anniversary basket, but instead, I'm laying out a suit for my man in the casket.

When U tell a black man to rise, will it be for pleasure, pressure, or pain, ladies? What do U want to gain? Ask yourself. Black man, what do U want to hear? How do U want to rise? Don't tell me to whisper that little something in your wife's ear for that surprise.

Single black men, rise off your seat and stop being so cheap and holla at the single sisters.

Black Man Rise! Black Man Rise!

Directions

What would it take to save a black man's pride to let him know it's not about his lies but about his soul and salvation, his home or his home going? Where would his soul go to? What home, in the sky or down under?

Let's not get it twisted. We all have somewhere that we are going to go. U C, it's about our soul, which way we go. Up, down, look around. Don't U wonder if your homies made it over or under, so what R U waiting on? Tomorrow is not promised.

If U want to win, be born again. That's a way to win!

Why are U still sitting there? Walk, black man, walk. It's about your soul and your salvation your home or where U might call home.

Some people are not right, but that's all right there in Church trying to get it right so they can have the right soul for their home.

Walk and see on what choice you're going to make. Wait, which way are you going, right or left? Just don't be caught in the in between.

If you act right, you'll see the light!

Don't Apologize for Your Blessings

Don't apologize for your blessing but walk in them to show people that the Lord is still good to us, so let the haters hate; that will be their mistake that they will just have to intake.

If you know the Lord has blessed you with a new home, or a new job, or a baby, or cars, and diamonds, and furs, or blessed you with a man or woman.

DON'T APOLOGIZE!

Don't apologize or whatever you been believing for don't apologize, but realize all good things come from God, so hold your head up high and continue to walk in your blessing from up high.

DON'T APOLOGIZE!

You don't know what your neighbor sitting beside you had to:

Go thru

To get thru

Or walk thru

To talk thru

Pray thru

Fast thru

DON'T APOLOGIZE!

For their break thru. So, don't apologize if anyone agrees with today; say to yourself, "I'm not apologizing."

Faith Shakers

Your mission is your assignment, so I came to shake up some faith. Don't abort the mission or vision God has given you, especially if He has made provision for U to complete the assignment that has been given to U.

U C, your next assignment could be your family member, a co-worker, the church saints, or ain'ts.

Let me tell you, church, I understand my assignment. That's why I'm standing here doing this poem, because I almost let go, but for every mountain, God has kept me because of my faith, God favors me.

U C I have my father's DNA not to go MIA when I know I have not completed my assignment yet.

My assignment might not be yours, so stay in your lane. It takes some unique faith to get some unique blessings. I'm not talking about that elementary faith, but…

- *Some radical faith*
- *Drum beating faith*
- *Crazy faith*
- *Running faith*
- *That I can't stop praising him kind of faith*
- *That leap of faith brothers that would make you ask that single sister out on a date faith*
- *That paying your tithes and offering faith*
- *That Hebrews 11 faith*

- *That faith that would make you name your child Faith*
- *That shouting faith that makes you say Amen faith when the preacher is preaching*
- *That faith that would make you wave your hands in the air like you-just-don't-care kind of faith.*
- *That faith that would make you leave that chair-sitting ministry and join another ministry.*
- *That singing faith (Lord, do it for me right now)*

I'm not a preacher, just a poet, please know it
Church, what kind of faith do you have?

Generations Take Back

I'm coming to you from news channel 2024, where the talk on the street is old school is talking to the next generation.

What do we do with a generation population surrounded by a bunch of temptations? Do we put a band-aid on the explanation to cover up the Godly truth or give directions to them on what to do?

We need to teach them how to proclaim it, and explain it, and demonstrate it, in the word of God, that they don't need to be tolerated but celebrated on doing the works of God.

So, let's take back this generation. You see, this is a transforming situation from the heart to explain, so we won't look like counterfeit Christians being lame.

Old school, please tell this generation to apply the word of God, and don't lie on the works of God, and let this be an outreach to teach.

Old school, can we take a moment and put our minds on rewind when you would hear those old church songs like Walk with Me Lord or The Blood Still Works, Jesus Will Fix It.

Tell the next generation you're perfectly crafted one of a kind, an exclusive design that God had you in mind, so don't try to redesign it and re-name it, and call it a transgender, but can someone please tell Bruce Jenner that he should have run the spiritual race that says, this race is not giving to the swift but to the one who endures, maybe today he wouldn't be walking in stilettoes on the floor.

You see, God already knew how he wanted you, every hair strand. God knows every detail like it was already planned.

Old school, tell the next generation of sisters and brothers to love one another as you walk in this journey called life, snapping your fingers to a beat, tapping your feet, and wiggling your toes, and the sound of your voice, God had it already composed.

If you don't like this station identification too bad, 'cause I'm not scared of none of ya'll, because I'm coming from you live and in person you can't change this channel, only your mind.

So old school, let's take back this generation.

This is StyLysa reporting to you from news channel 2024. Jesus, I turn it back over to you, oops! You already have it.

Girlfriends, the Sistas

When you're looking for a laugh, there goes Jo, or should I say jokes on us with Jo, because hanging around Jo that's just how it goes, we often wonder why she had to go, but God has a plan that no man can rearrange or change.
Jo just made it home a place of rest a place to dry all her tears where she has no more fears, because she fought the good fight of faith.

Jo has always been the leader of the bunch of the sista girls whether it was do your hair like this, or that looks ruff, I know you're not wearing that stuff.
Now in a sense I guess she's still leading we might say in our hearts that's not right, but she fought the fight, and that's alright.

When I think of my friend girl now I don't see her in the world doing hand dance because I know she stopped that long ago, I know that her hand dance just turned into God's praise dance now Jo, I know you had to go, but some things I know are just God's business I truly say you are a girlfriend of transition from us dancing on the dance floor to us praising the Lord for His glory and might.
Girl Friends SHE FOUGHT THE FIGHT now to my other friends and sisters Janet, Angie, Shaun, Sharon, Yvette, her spirit is up high, so tell the rest some things are just God's Business… RIP JO!

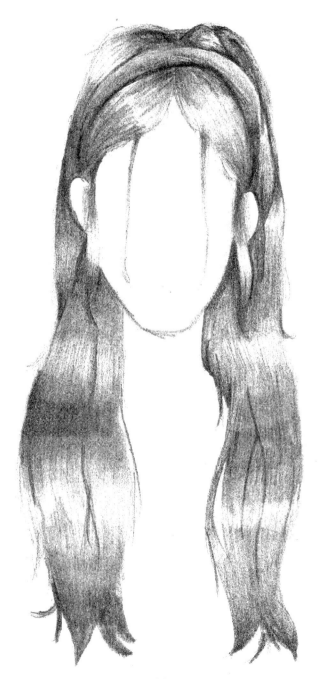

A Black Woman's Weave and Wigs

Men, please be careful of a black woman's hair; you see, you'll never know if it's a weave or wig or her own hair, sisters wear it all, short, tall, slim, biscuit thick, young age, middle age, or season saints, please don't touch a black woman's hair while in transition of a new hairdo.

I see a sista carrying a bag of hair headed towards the beauty salon. Sista girl, is that a bag of hair to achieve a glorious weave or big wig.

Hey sista girl, is that a #2 that's about to be your new do?

Sista wait you drop some hair you might want to go back and get it straight.

Oh! Here come another sista trying to achieve that glorious wig, or weave.

You men might want to get back she's not finish sewing in that #2 yak.

All look now a sista to sista she's all finish to be picked up now but wait I hear a phone right, oh! oh! oh! it's your mother she's now finished, here comes another.

What a woman would to do achieve that glorious weave or wig. I hope you brothers understand there will be another sista to be picked up with a glorious weave now get back until that # 2 yak is down her back.

I -can-do-bad-all-by-myself

*You men come into my life making me false promises, but what they
don't know they just step to a woman who has already been told she is
fearfully and wonderfully made.*

*Because my daddy already told me who I was, and who I am, so when
you step to me hummmm!! I'll know who you are, because I don't have
an identity crisis.*

For – I- know- who- I am!

*I know where I been, who I did, who did me and who won't do me
period.*

*You're in and out of my life, in and out my life but that's alright
because God already told me he'll never leave me or forsake me, so keep
it moving because the only promises that means anything right about
now is God's promises and not a man's.*

*You see, you'll never have my heart because my daddy already told me
to guard it, so right now, it's under lock and key, and you don't have a
key or a clue.*

*You see, this is not a story about a diary of a mad black woman who is
not easily broken, wearing stilettos, trying to get out of the ghetto.*

*I have a family that prays together while still going to my family
reunions, keeping Madea out of jail from something you're trying to do
because*

*I -can-do-all-by-myself, without a man doing disappearing acts in
my life.*

*Ooohh!! Please don't let me set if off up in, so talk to me, it's not all
about the Benjamins or bringing down the house, so please don't step
to me like an American Gangster, from the training days, because King
Kong don't have nothing on me.*

I – am- a-woman- thou- art- loose, just waiting to exhale!

It takes a village to protect a child

To discover your child's potential is one of a parent's things to do that becomes essential in raising a child.

The Bible tell us in Proverbs 22 to train up a child and the way he should go, and when he becomes old, he will not depart from it.

That requires us to love them, not leave them, to teach them not to torture them or to abandon them, but to keep them safe and alive.

It takes a village to protect a child, so we as parents have to stay in our right mind while we discipline our kids and beat their behinds and teach our kids to tell the devil to flee to get thee behind me.

When our kids are not around us, are they trained to call on the name of Jesus? And not Tyrone or Taisha in a time of need, but to call Jesus even down on bending knees.

We know they're going to make mistakes because we did, but can your child come to you in a time of trouble or need and you both take it to the Lord down on bending knees.
The school system tried to take prayer out of school, but not out of our kids; TRAIN UP A CHILD.
We tell our kids nursery rhymes at a small age, about Jack and Jill went up a hill to get a pail of water, but why not tell them about Jesus who went up a hill called Calvary?

Ingredients of a Cookbook or Bible

When we want a recipe, we open up a cookbook for the ingredients to put something together to make something work.

Why not take the Bible as a cookbook to put some things together in our life to make our family, finance, and faith work?
A cookbook will allow you to taste the finish results, but the Bible will let you taste and see as you're putting the ingredients together for the finish results.

Some ingredients the heat will be turned up in your life, but there will also be a cooling down point where the heat's not a bad thing always, just look at it as touch not this anointed and remember sometimes the heat has to be turned up in your life to get you to go to the Bible to taste and see His goodness.

The Bible says it will be alright if just the ingredients of life.

What's cooking in your life?

Mighty Men of Valor

The essential of a father's love is that a son and daughter see a potential of being loved because God is love even if it's a hug from a father that appears to be a thug. So, the results are in, you have different kinds of fathers out there, so let me describe them to you.

You have biological fathers, grandfathers, godfathers fathers, single parent fathers, gay fathers, oops! Hold up, wait a minute, those 2 dads in the home, that's not cool because there's nothing in the Bible saying that's been approved.

There should always be a time when a son and daughter can reminisce in their minds of a father being there and not missing all the time. So, a salute to the Dads for being there to make the family last whether you had a rocky or ruff pass.

Thank God for the fathers who didn't leave but had in your minds, I will trust God and believe. You see, men, God has made you 1st. I often wonder why! Is it because of your strong spine? I ask the Divine; some ladies call you fine, ummmmm! I don't deny it, but I look a little deeper from within because you are often asked are you your brother's keeper.

Yes, you are so don't go far, because I see a protector, a navigator, a father, a husband, a son, a military man, a business owner, a Pastor, a blue-collar worker, C E O, don't you knowww there's no limit to the mighty men of valor.

Back in slavery, you were a threat to the white man, but God has a plan for the strong black seed that you are yes indeed, you can go far because of who you are.

So, continue to be there for the seed that's growing up for you to water from your root, whether it's a flower of a girl, or yeah that's my boy.

Ladies, can we applaud them, please!
You are the seed we need to multiply in victory.
So, continue to wear the helmet, the shield, the buckler, and to hold up your sword, as you hold up your hands to give God all the praise, might men of valor, because the steps of a good man are ordered by the Lord, Psalms 37:23.

To God be all the Glory!

Misunderstood

*On this journey called life, you will meet people that will find you a
little misunderstood. What do you do?*

Hmmm!

*How about another introduction and re-introduce yourself to make it
all good in the sister hood.*

*Not everyone is going to like you or myself liking them, but that's ok.
Rodney King put it like this, "can't we all just get along," as we walk
by each other and others being misunderstood, whether wearing a tight
girdle, still trying to get over that misunderstood hurdle, by doing that
we can make the devil mad because he thought he won that fight, but
God always get the victory and will make all things right.*

*So, who am I fearfully and wonderfully made? Who are you, the same!
Fearfully and wonderfully made.*

*Misunderstood sometimes can make things reveal itself, by keeping
things on the real.*

*In a sisterhood, trying to make it all good where superstars really do
shine without bussing open that good bottle of wine.*

Veterans Day

Being in the army of the Lord is the Highest Rank!

Remember When

There was a time when we all looked back and said to ourselves I remember when I was broke, depressed, lonely, divorced, on drugs, pimping, crying, hopeless, homeless, hustling, we all had our time of saying, I remember when if you haven't said it yet, live long enough it's coming.

If we don't say it then how can we say, thank you, Lord for bringing me out of my remember when times, and turning my emotions to devotions.

When there are storms in life walk closer to Christ. Sometimes your mess is your message of life, because He said He'll never leave you or forsake you, so be a victor and not a victim of life and know that you can't have change without a challenge.

It's a pop quiz time of life, it's when we come out and pass the test of our trails for we all are students of life know that education informs us, but Jesus Christ transforms us; what grade will U get? Will you fail and stay back to go thru that test again, or will you pass and go to the next level of life and take a new quiz of life?
Just remember, it's just the I remember a time of life to say thank you, Lord, for my remember when times of life, so how I can give my testimony.

Run the Race

Truth be told we're all running a race, Sha'Carri Richardson race is just called Track and Field, while some of our race is called family, jobs, struggles, health, depression, oppression, in this Journey called life.

Being in the public eye can be a blessing and a curse, but when you know something about Bible verse like Ecclesiastes 9:11, now go run and tell that in 10.72 seconds, because I'm That Girl! That would put it out there on paper, and pen please hear or read this Poem till the end.

With a voice to be heard, I'm a different kind of Poet, you better know it.

Sha'Carri Richardson go run that race with God's G-Race! TGBATG

Soap Opera Life

We only have one life to live
So, we won't end up in a general hospital
Weather we are the haves or, the have nots.
With all my children who might be the young and the restless

Wondering if loving you is wrong and thinking they're the bold and
the beautiful with no passion for today.
So, get into the presence of the Lord as the world turns.
Continue to walk toward the guiding light who is Jesus Christ.

Now, take up your cross and walk!

Sound the Alarm

In Joel 2:1, sound the alarm and blow the trumpet for the day of the Lord is coming. Moving forward in today's society, sound the alarm means something is happening in the atmosphere.

Whether it's a siren from a fire truck going down the road, or a police car, or a utility vehicle doing some work, please don't fear because one of these vehicles is near; help is on the way, don't you hear it's a sound of the alarm when something is going on.

This invitation for the people here today, because of their occupation should be celebrated with the highest utmost of appreciation, so we thank you! Roger that! Copy that! 10- 4! Ya know your language lingo! So here we go!

Firemen, policemen, and utility workers, I need ya to remember this poet today, so if my house catch on fire, ya hired to put the fire out.

Policemen, if I get pulled over for a ticket for driving too fast, I'm going to need some grace, so when I roll down the window, I need y'all to remember this face.

Utility workers, that song Teddy Pendergrass made back in the day, turn off the lights, pay no attention because when those storms come, we are waiting for it to be restored for those without power for the next couple of hours. Do what you do best and give us some power.

I pray that the Lord continue to keep you safe in your line of duty and to know that your labor is not in vain, and that needs to have a sound of its own appreciation, now copy that!

Stepping High Into My Destiny

Hey, gurlll, what's going on? Oh whattt! Really! Well, do you know who you are? Or should I say whose you are, U see if you don't know you better ask somebody. You see you never connect with your future until you disconnect from your pass, so don't go off and roam just hang up the phone and call Jesus on his main line and tell him what you want, ok lady I'll talk to you later gurl, **Ya! She really needs help to step high into her destiny.**

Let me tell you what people would try to do and being transparent, people would try to keep me in my past, but that didn't last I know JESUS I MY SUPPLIER NOT MY DENIER Philippians 4:19 tells me so! Because, I seen single, married, and divorce and now I'm single with a voice for the Lord who I truly adore.

So, thank you Lord, for not leaving me in my storms, while I had to get down on bended knees praying trying to get to my destiny.

Along with that came praying for my enemies (hmmmm)! Now, I just thank my enemies knowing God will prepare a table before me in the presence of them, and not a meal you see they thought they can break me, but all they did was make me pray a little harder, praise a little harder, worship a little harder and those were all just for starters.

Just like the rapper Hammer, I'm too legit to quit right now in this fight because, I know Jesus died for me he wouldn't lie to me, because I'm a work in progress stepping high into my destiny and telling the others goodbye who not supposed to go with me. I know I have to still have to change some of my ways, because we're living in the last days, but God got a hold of me in this step with destiny, now ask your neighbor are you stepping high towards your destiny. You see ladies this is our story for God to get all the glory, as we continue to step high into our destiny.

The Kitchen in The Black Family

The kitchen is the family gathering spot for cooking food to cooking hair, or press and curls, I should say they would say back in the day. Take soul food, for instance. The family would meet up every Sunday and cook at Momma Jo's house and eat.

Family time to me is watching our history to our future on TV, from Roots to Run's House, to Soul Food, and many more. For instance, Momma Jo was the rock of that family, while Barack is the head of his family, and now the white house for that season, but we know Jesus Christ is the real rock of all our families.

Makes me want to holla and throw up both my hands!

As I watched the Baltimore riots and look at these people stealing, and setting fires, if they only knew they are making it harder for someone to have jobs available for them to be hired.

But I see 3 black women coming to the forth front to resolve this demonstration situation, and to stop all this confrontation and devastation for this generation.

Such as, U. S. Attorney General Loretta Lynch, I hope she is ready, because her job won't be a cinch, and State Attorney Marilyn Mosby, prosecutor, young and in charge. This will be a true test, because she just made 6 arrests.

Mayor Stephanie Blake, who put the armed forces out there late, but still came thru, and got Baltimore on track to stop all the confusion and delusions that the people are having.

So, the people won't think they can destroy a city, and stop all that self-hate, and get there mind straight now here comes the other states.

March on New York, Boston, Philly, as people join together and not acting so silly, but to stop the scrutiny in the vicinity for the need of today's society.

Just know our focus is not on the word thug, but on the resolution of Freddie Gray's trial, so at the end, we can hopefully stand up and give each other hugs, and be proud. Baltimore is a proud city with a great industrial past, knowing that this rioting will not last.
This will go down in Baltimore history of being no mystery of how these 3 women had stand firm with power that took hours, to get Baltimore back on track, now where is CNN and the big news channel how about reporting that!

The {-} Dash in Life

We all will have a dash in life you know the time you were born and the time you die, or shall I say come alive when we are up high.

The dash is the in-between from one time period to the next when you look at your in-between what do you see? God can see were your dash of life where you will be, living more for Him or the world, what will your dash tell about your life?

The dash is your story life of how you lived, did you take the time to give or maybe to forgive? will your dash tell the story of someone dashing thru life with no cares in the world as through you was dashing in the snow with nowhere to go.

Will your dash show a sincere person or a sinful person will your dash show a cheerful person? Will your dash show an abusive or a kindhearted person, or a prayer warrior, or a peace maker a counterfeit Christian or a countable Christian, will your dash show you how you were pressing for heaven in your life, or horror in your life?

Please believe we all will have a dash in our life. What story will yours tell? Were you a good and faithful servant, or a good and faithful deserter? What can people say about your dash? Were you an encourager or a discourager? Did you know how to win in life or just give in to life? Did you try to succeed? Or did you settle for less? Did you have a good marriage with you and your boo? Or made no effort and stayed single without a clue? Were you confident in the things of life or cockeyed in the life of things? How do you see it?

What it boils down to is it's not what people say about the dash in your life; it's about what God says about the dash, so what will yours tell? Will your dash tell the story before the glory of someone that had to abstain, sustain, contain, retain, reframe, or maintain in the word of God.

Look at your dash while you are still living!

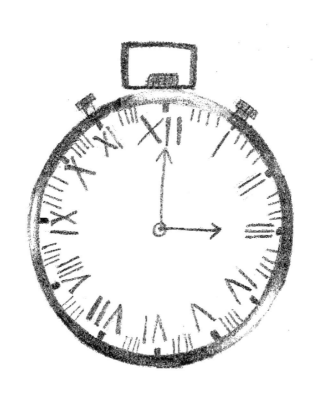

Time

There is a time!

A time to die

A time to tell the truth

But not to lie

There is a season for everything we go thru in life

Why not raise our praise

To stop our delays!

The Pain, The Process, to His Presence

When all you see is your pain, then you lose sight of me, let the pain go, and you'll see all of me.

My presence takes the pain away, so the process will begin in you to take the pain away, so remove your veil and let me reveal life in a different way that you would stay in me. People will know that you were in my presence.

For I will be all over you because the pain has pressed out of you now the process has begun in you thru you, and out of you, so walk in my presence for where there is no more pain, but peace.

Some will ask you, and you will say for my God has not forsaken me, but some might hear I have just taken thee to the next level in me.

Whoever will be in my presence for there you will find peace in me and no more pain.

For I am your

Advil

Tylenol

Motrin

Dayquil

Nightquil

Alka-Seltzer

I am the medicine with no FEE

What am I trying to say to all my believers I am the pain reliever, for you don't need to read the bottle for your next dose; just pick up your Bible for an overdose of me. That's where the healing starts.

The Take Back Time For Color Girls

Taste and see it's going to be all of me bringing my words, getting U out of your seat, and standing on your feet, because I am not sugar - coating nothing, but keeping it raw cause it's all about the words from pen to paper, and I'm not breaking nobodies' law.

I'm a color girl who's taking back my stuff I had enough!

I'm taking back my thoughts, because your talk doesn't line up with your walk, so you're out of time and out of your mind, but don't forget there's still one more out there with your blood running thru her veins.

U C your words would make a baby hungry, but your actions would make her burp.

Men, you can't participate in this, so just sit back and take notes and wait 2 C the color girls do their thing.

Who am I?

"The Quiet Storm"

Who R U?

Out of time!

A Street Life (a parent's cry)

Don't expect a thug to give you a holy hug when he hasn't been dipped in the baptismal pool because he's still out there on that drug tip. He hasn't heard that Jesus died for our blood because he still out there with stains of blood on his car hood from the gang banging in the hood.

Pants saggy making a jail statement, not knowing the history of saggy pants could be his future, if he was not so disillusional from the drugs he's taking, that could be the conclusion of a mother's fear, to stand over her son with last drops of tears, the street made him a promise of a quick fix of a money situation, because he wasn't able to stay in school for his graduation.

Stop your crying, friend here come the doctor with a report only to hear your son will live with only 50% body support, U see the streets took half of him, but God says I have all of him with the rehabilitation of his mind, giving me back my Bible and praise time.

That boy will take up his cross and walk again, because I have given him breath to talk again U see when he was walking the streets of D.C. I was really showing him all of me, that carry a 9 mm gun, that would land him here in the hospital without the street life of fun. My friend, God says He hears your cries, so dry your eyes, because he can do it for you because it did it for my friend's son. **"True story."**

The Witness Program

Sometimes you have to open up and tell what the Lord has done for
you, and yes, that means your business, your deliverance, your past,
and how you passed the test to let somebody know they're not all
alone in their fight.

To be a part of the witness program, we are all being watched by
somebody we might not know by whom, but it can be just in our
actions that cause the attractions that can make a difference, and
sometimes not saying a word is a silent witness in the witness
program.

To be a part of the witness program, it can be in your clothes, music,
your company where you laid your head, and in whose bed.

Ladies, the utterance of your lips, or the walk in your hips!

Men in your bi-ceps, or your Bible concepts, your rap, or who you tap!

You see in Revelations 12:11 says they overcame Him by the blood of
the Lamb, and by the word of their testimony.

So, why R U sitting down on what we use to be like if we're not there
anymore, because I know we have some former;

Pimps, drug user, child abusers, alcoholics, drug dealers, cussing
bandits, prostitutes, spouse beaters or cheaters, and that's just naming
a few that might be sitting out there in the Church Sunday pew.

When are U going to join the Witness Program to help somebody to let
the know they're not all alone in their fight?

I'm standing here as a member of the Witness Program to let you
know how God can use anybody.

Are you a part of the Witness Program?

Your Mess Is Your Message of Ministry

Mess - *something that is not going right (a compound blend), but when will it end? Webster says it's of confusion, chaos.*

Jesus will take this compound blend and put it to an end to get the message out, but that's just the first part of the word messages, so please don't get up and depart because this isn't the end; the 2nd part is age.

Age- *a particular point or time of one's life, whether you're an infant, youth, or adult. You're attached to the word age now. When you start going thru some mess in your life at whatever stage or age you're at, just remember, that's your message of ministry at that age is for that season.*

Stop looking for the why me, Lord, reason, so the next time some mess comes up in your life, and it will come, just look at the age you're at.

Put the mess-n-age together and know it's a part of ministry in your life.

Unmask the Scriptures

Listen! Can you hear? Listen, can you hear that? The pages of the Bible are turning. Cell phones and tablets are opening up.

The people are starting to unmask the scriptures again, this time to another level, another realm. They are actually reading and meditating on them. Look at that. Break thrus and the testimonies are now coming true.

Look! Can you see it? The masks are coming off the people. They are starting to see 2ⁿᵈ Chronicles 7:14.

If my people, which are called by my name, shall humble themselves, and pray and seek my face, and turn from their wicked way then will I hear from heaven and will heal their land.

Church, are you his people, are you humble, can you pray and seek his face, are you ready for the turn, can you hear? do you want to see the land heal?

Then let me finish my reveal. You see, God had a plan, and as we unmask the mask off our faces and start to fill the church building place to raise our praise.

People are coming from out the church building and praising the Lord, inside and outside the hospital doors. Did you see it? Take another look because I've seen it all over Facebook.

You see long before the coronavirus, there was always Corinthians', Colossians, and Chronicles.

Some called it Rona, but I say come here, Romans.

Unmask the Scriptures-2

While you had people looking for cans of Lysol, Leviticus was still available to you.

While you were looking for hand sanitizers, Hebrews was still there waiting on you.

While you were looking for toilet tissue, 1st and 2nd Timothy's was available to you.

When you were looking for Clorox, Colossian was close by you.

While material things were running low or out. The word of God was still open 24/7; our common ground should be going to heaven.

While you were looking for meat in the stores, there goes Malachi, Matthews, Mark, Michal at your door. Tell that to the people forming supermarket lines and at home bored.

While you were in the stores and water was running low, the living water never ran out because he's able.
I know he can do it. He said he'd help us thru it.

Yeah! I said it! I meant it! I'm here to represent it!
Are you totally unmasked now??????

Closing Prayer

I Prayed

that all the readers were blessed

Spiritually

Practically

Humorously

In a soulful kind of way

For the soul

From a Soul Sista

Made in the USA
Columbia, SC
11 March 2024

32474926R00043